Adult Coloring Book

Africa Wild Life

Bambang Wisudyantoro

cannonzhooter@gmail.com

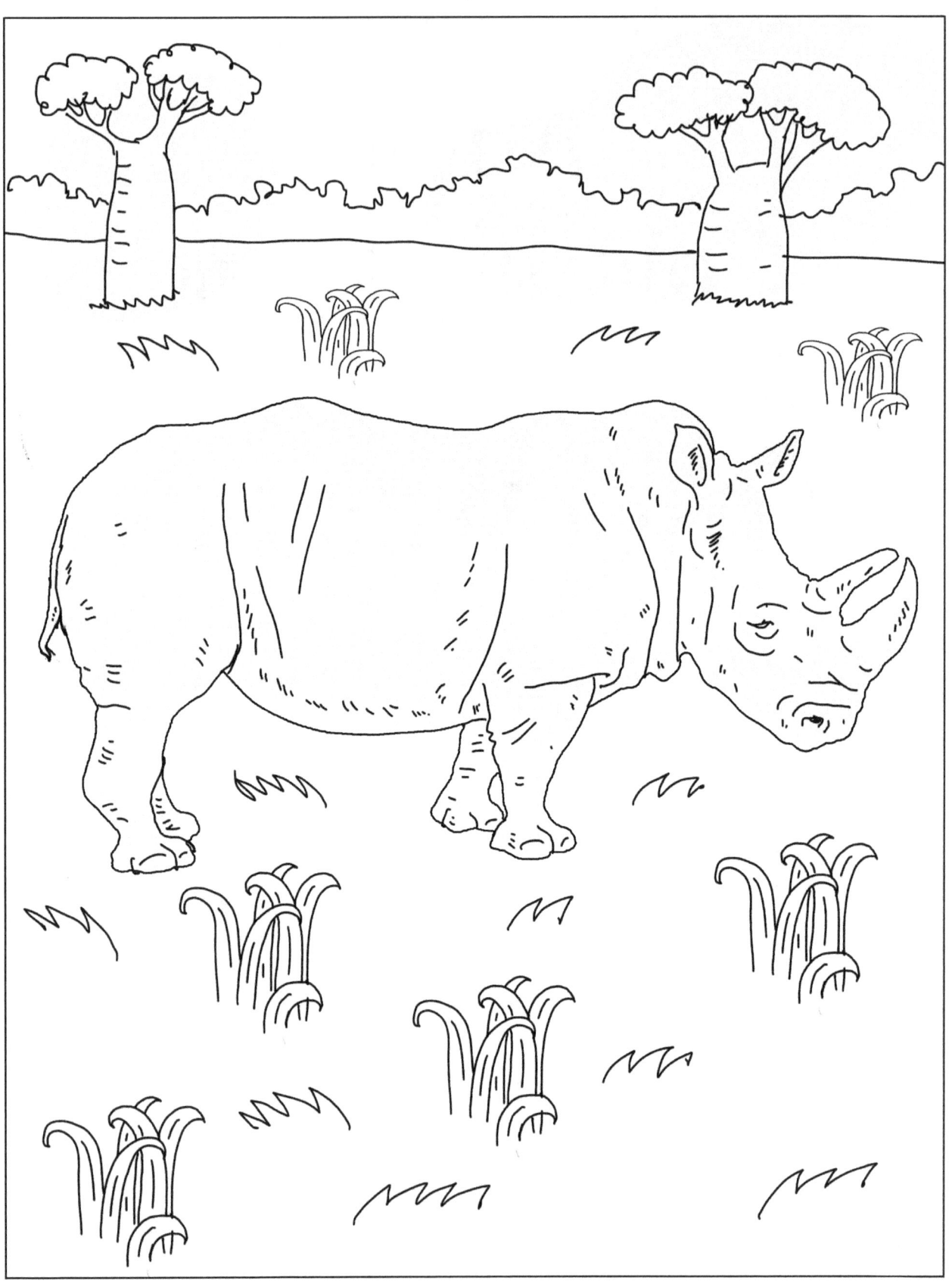

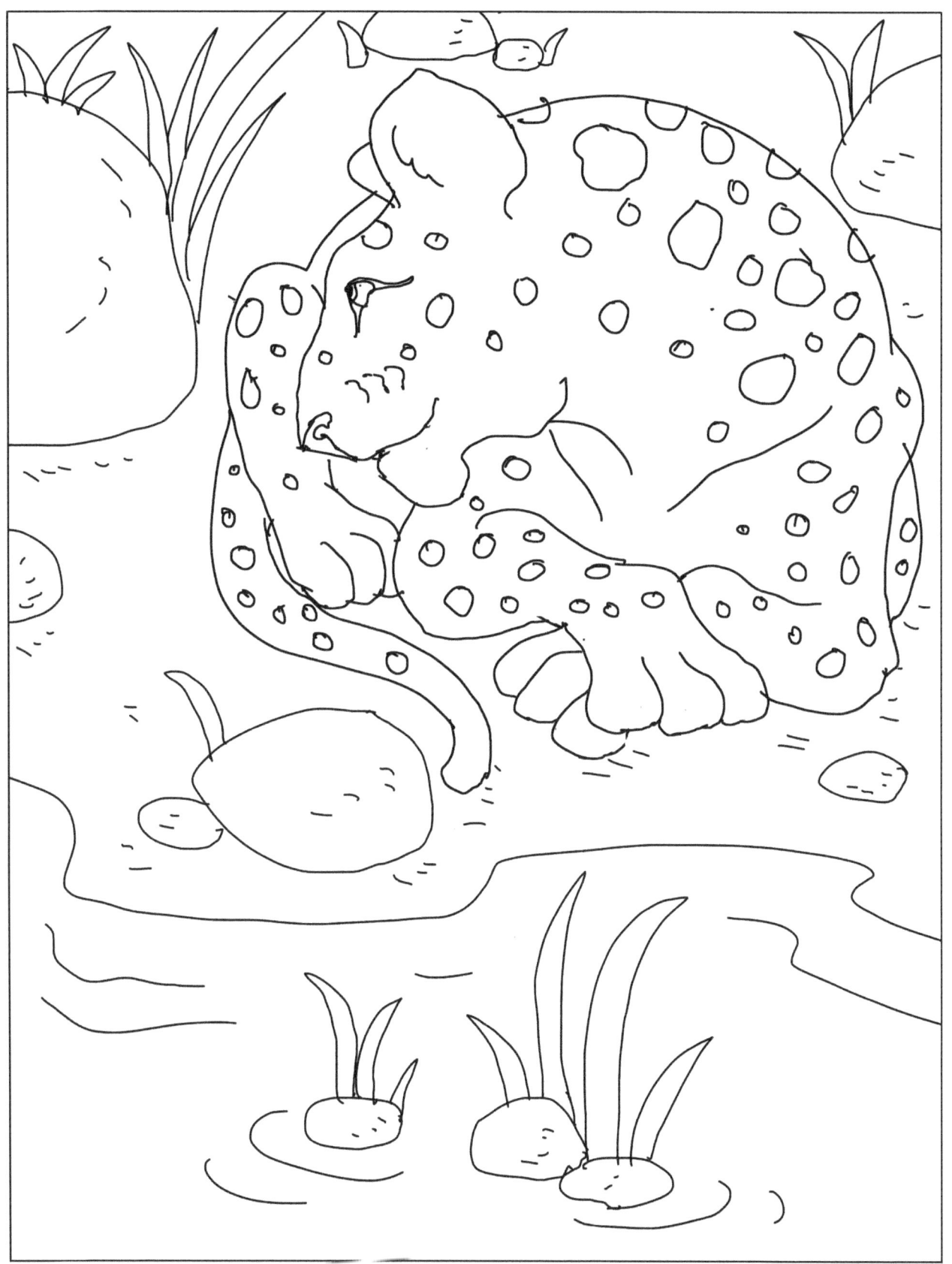

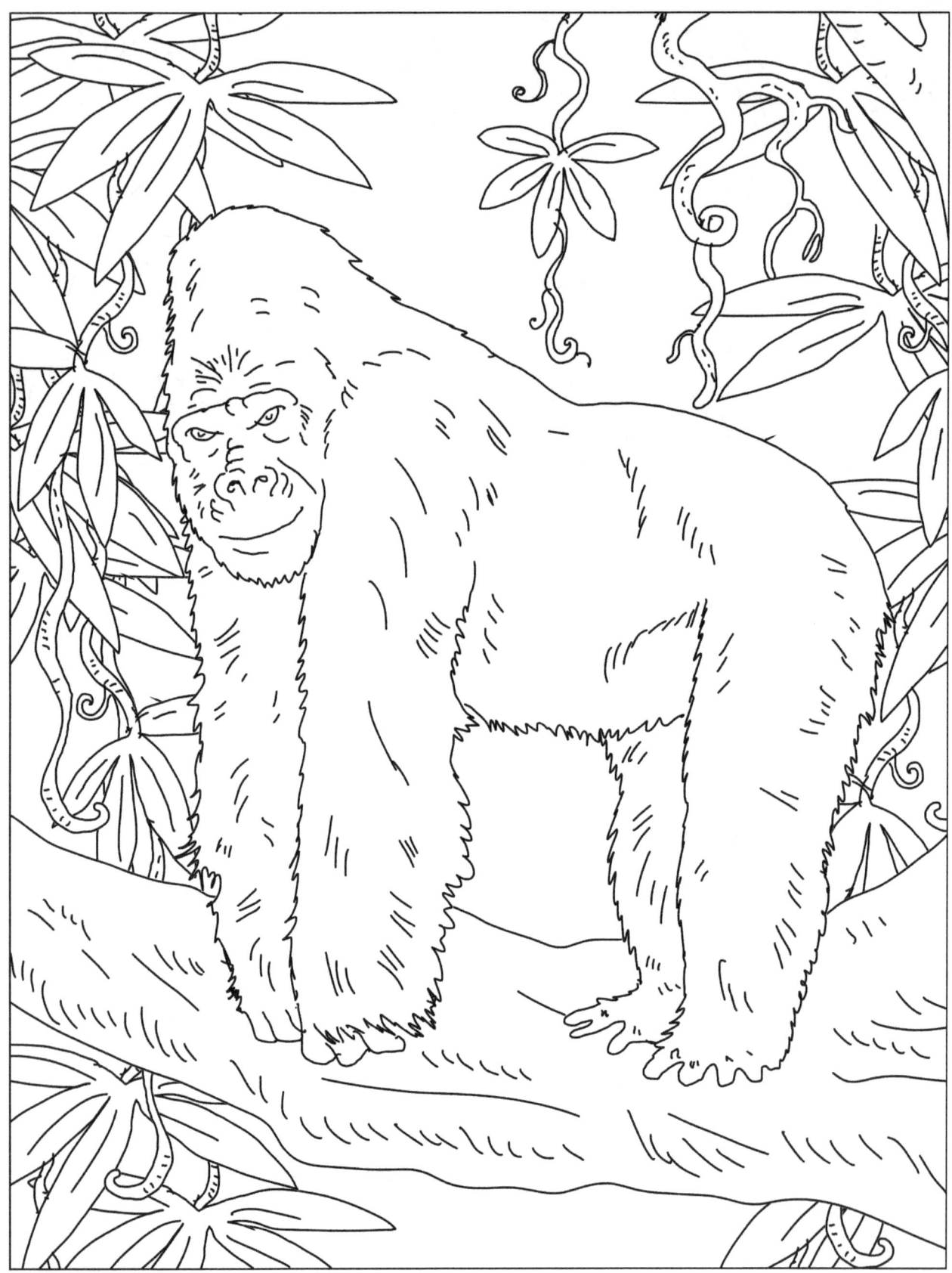

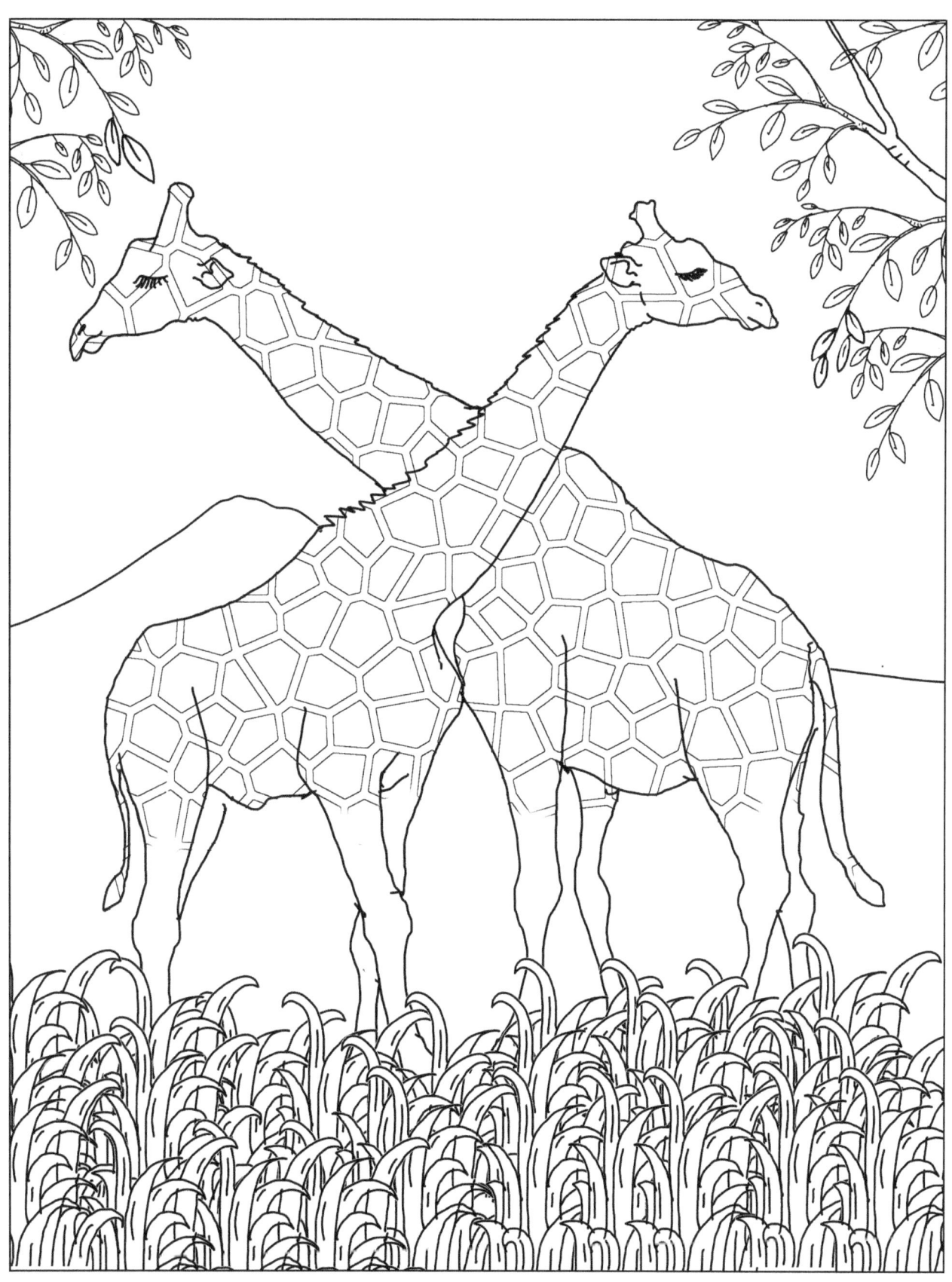

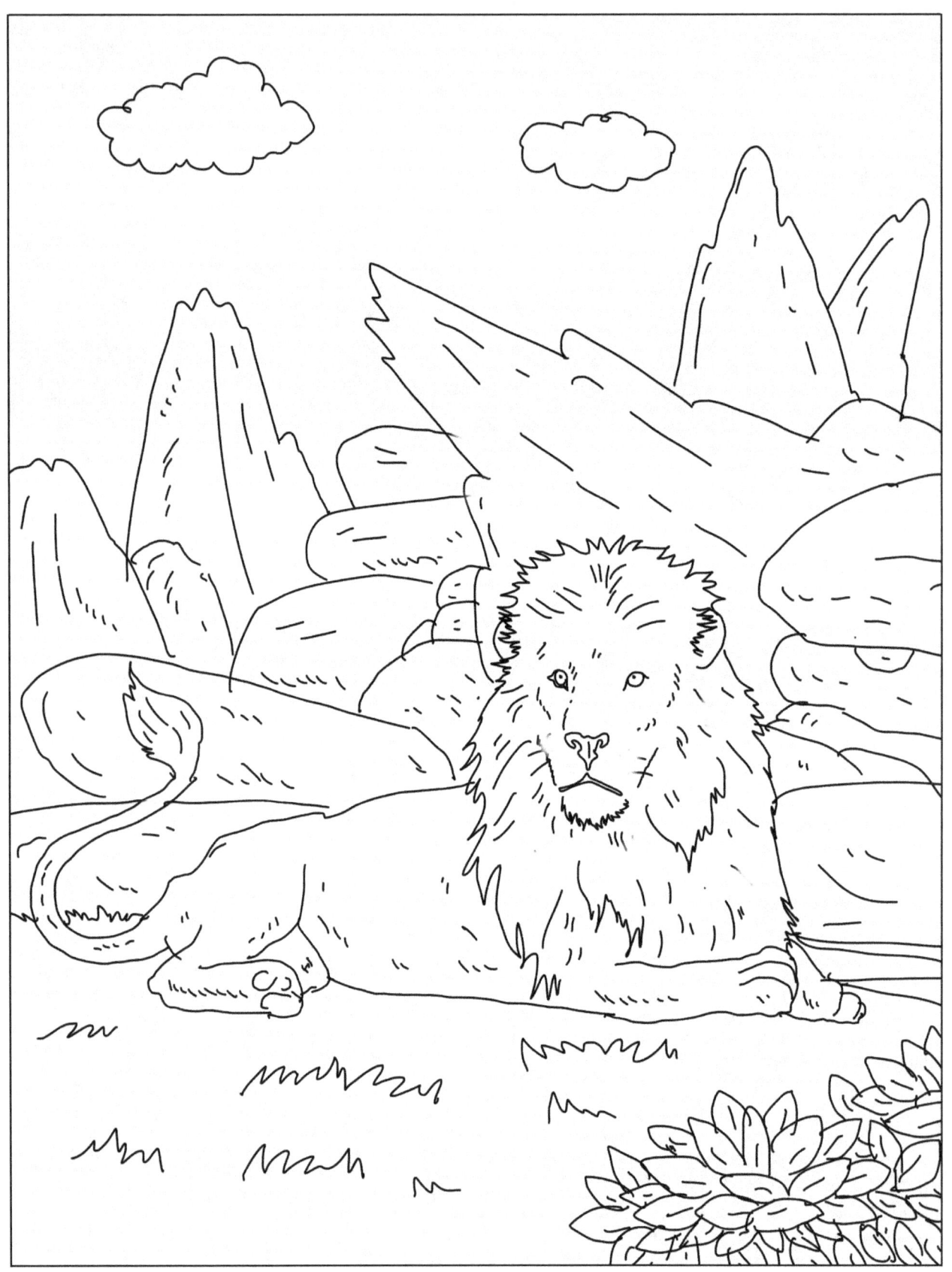

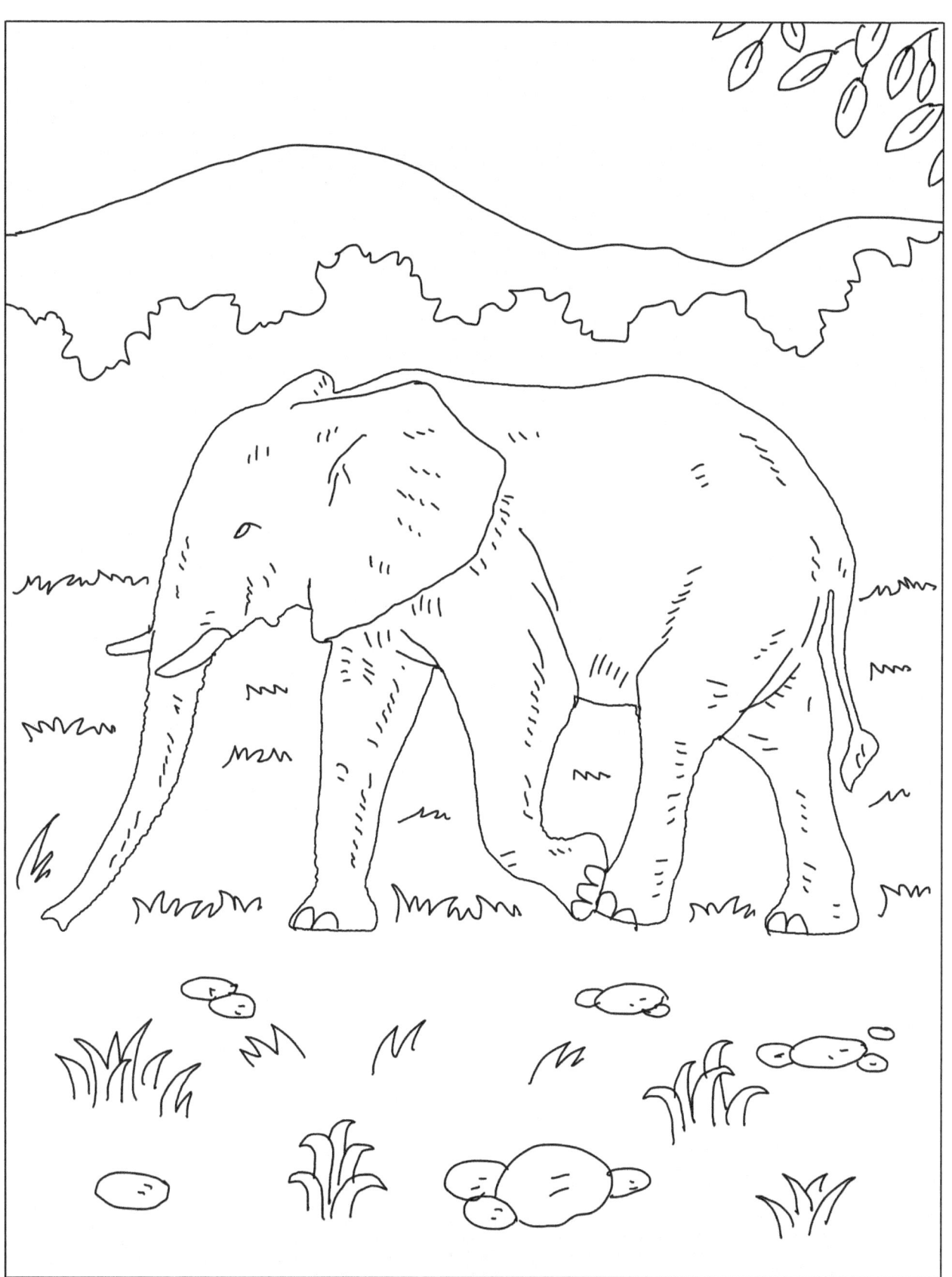

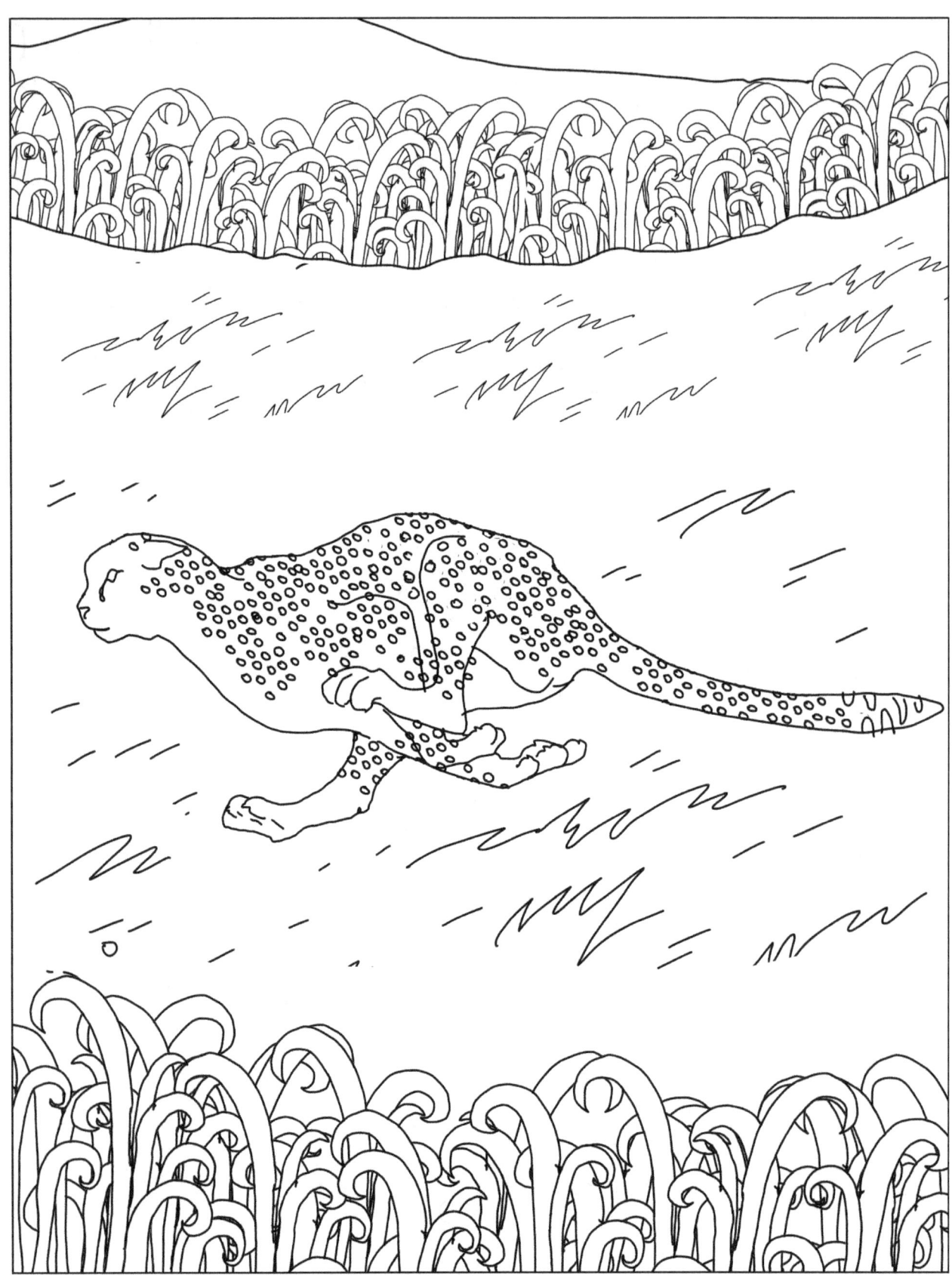

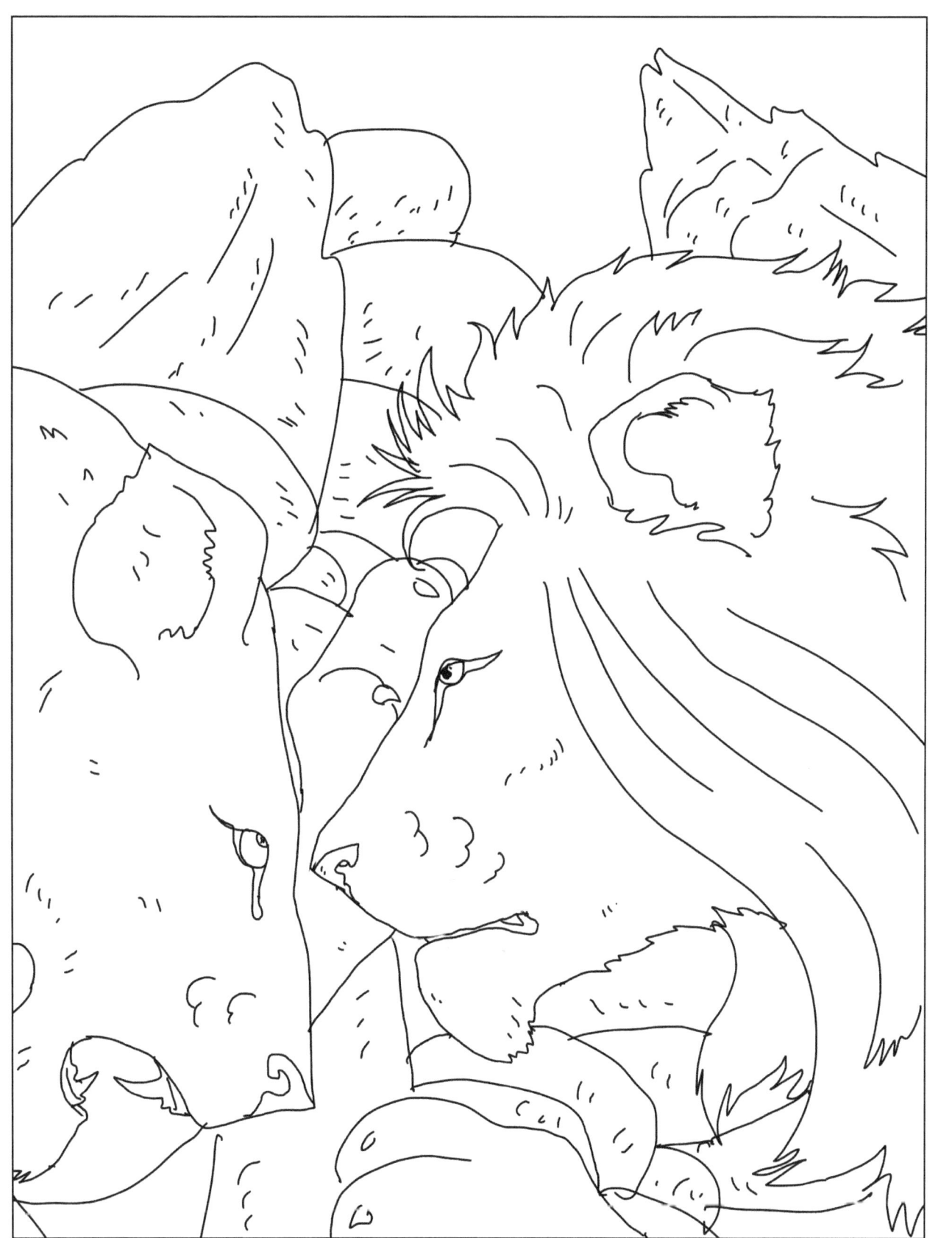

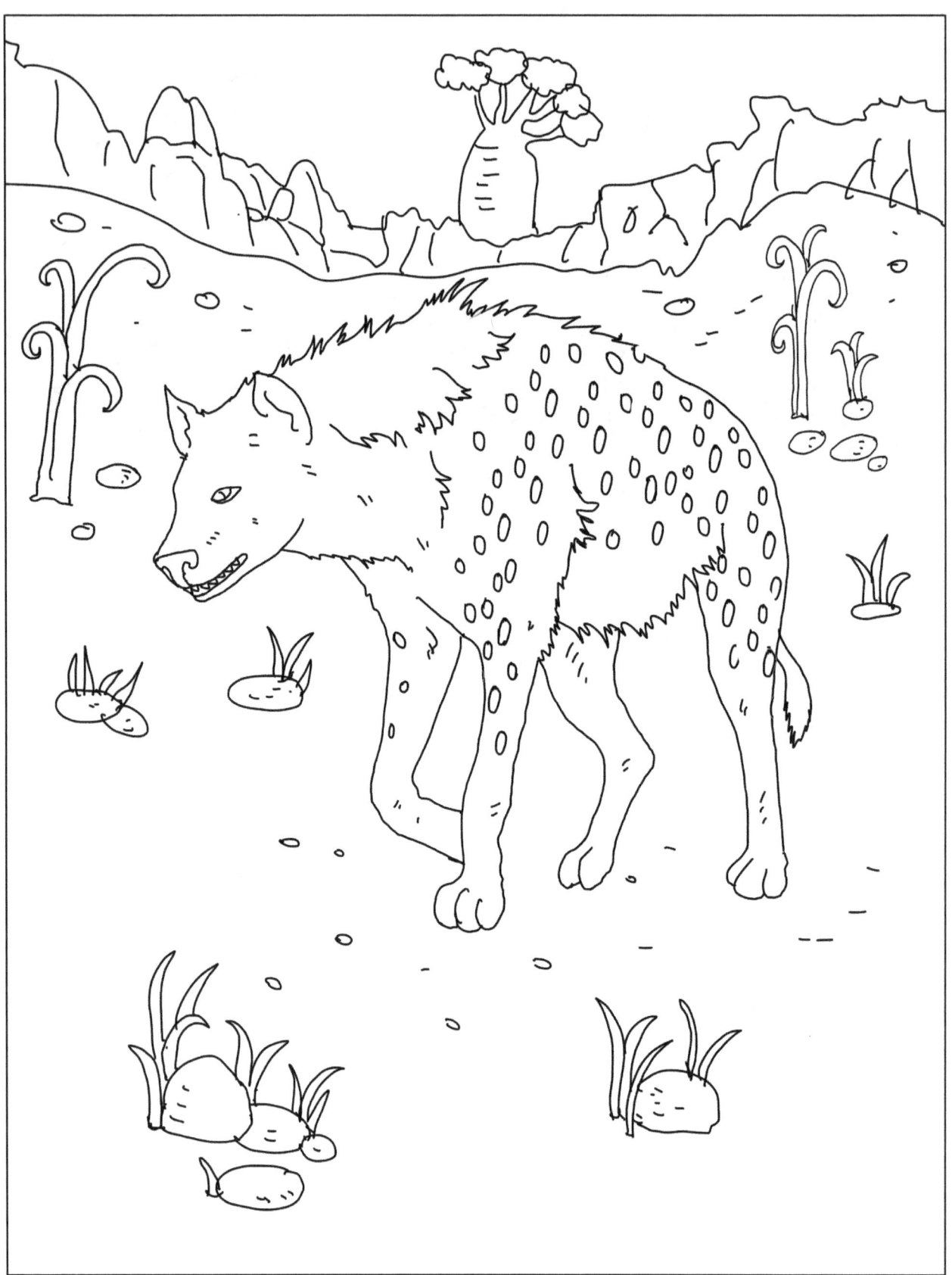

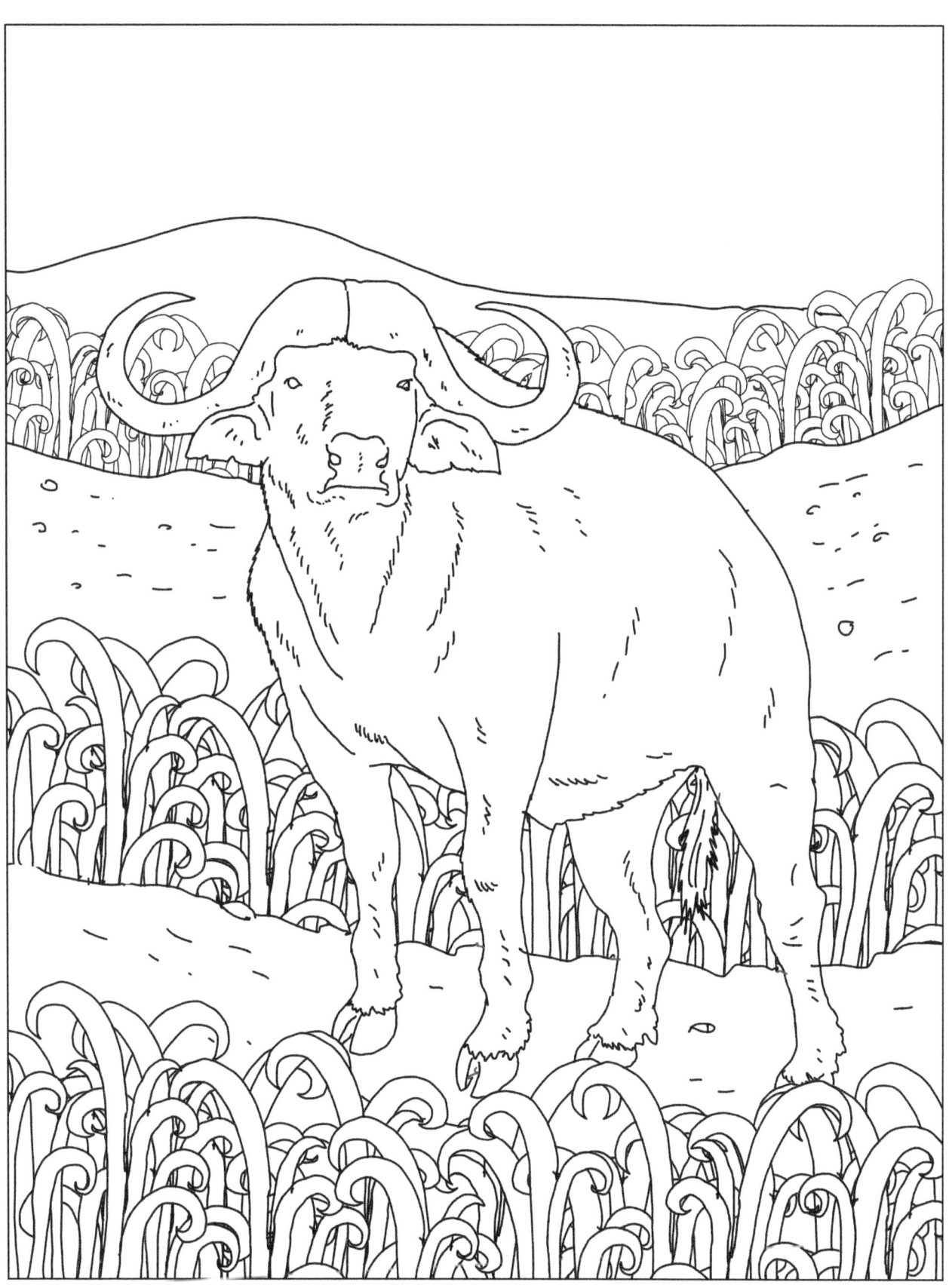

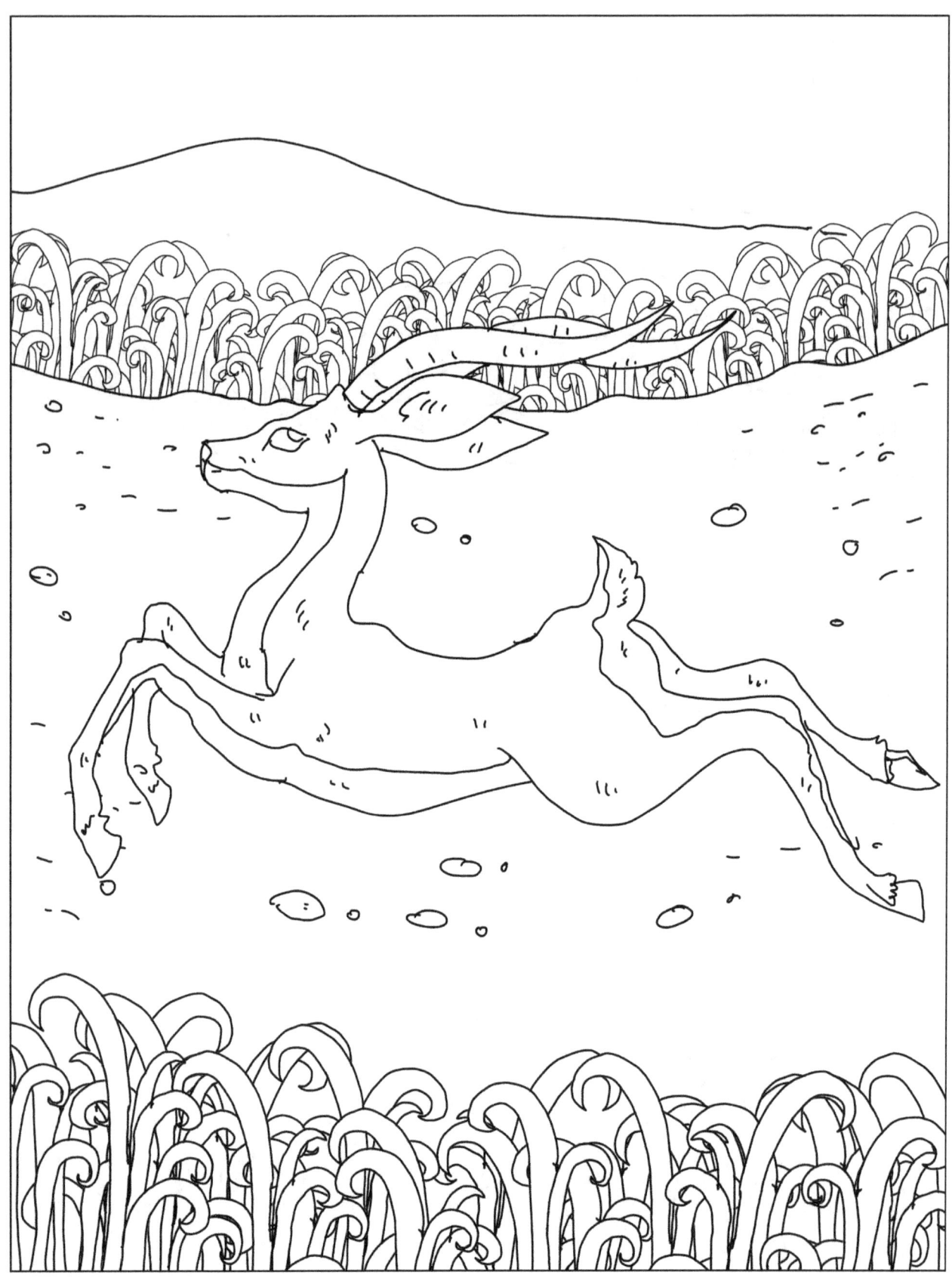

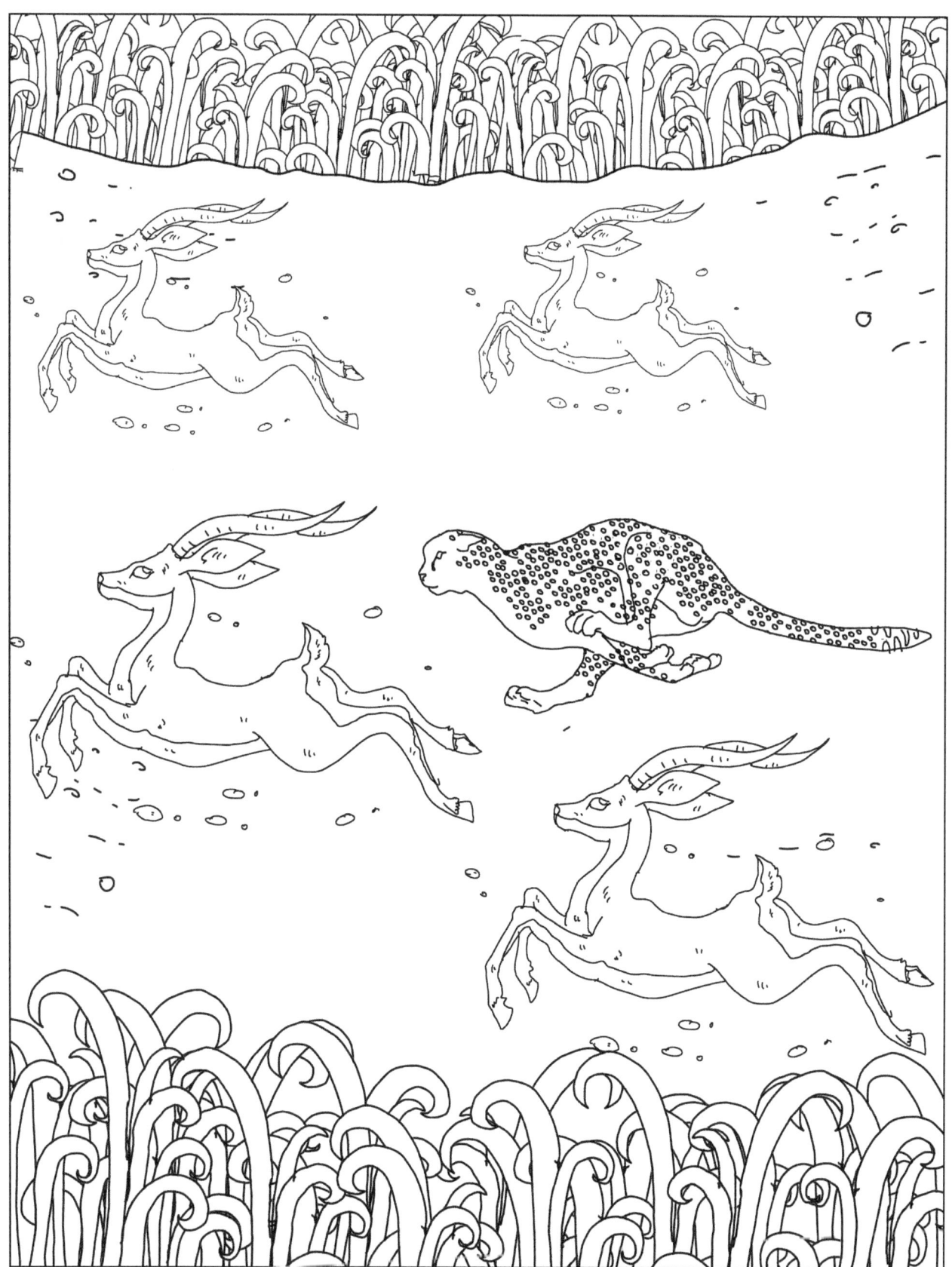

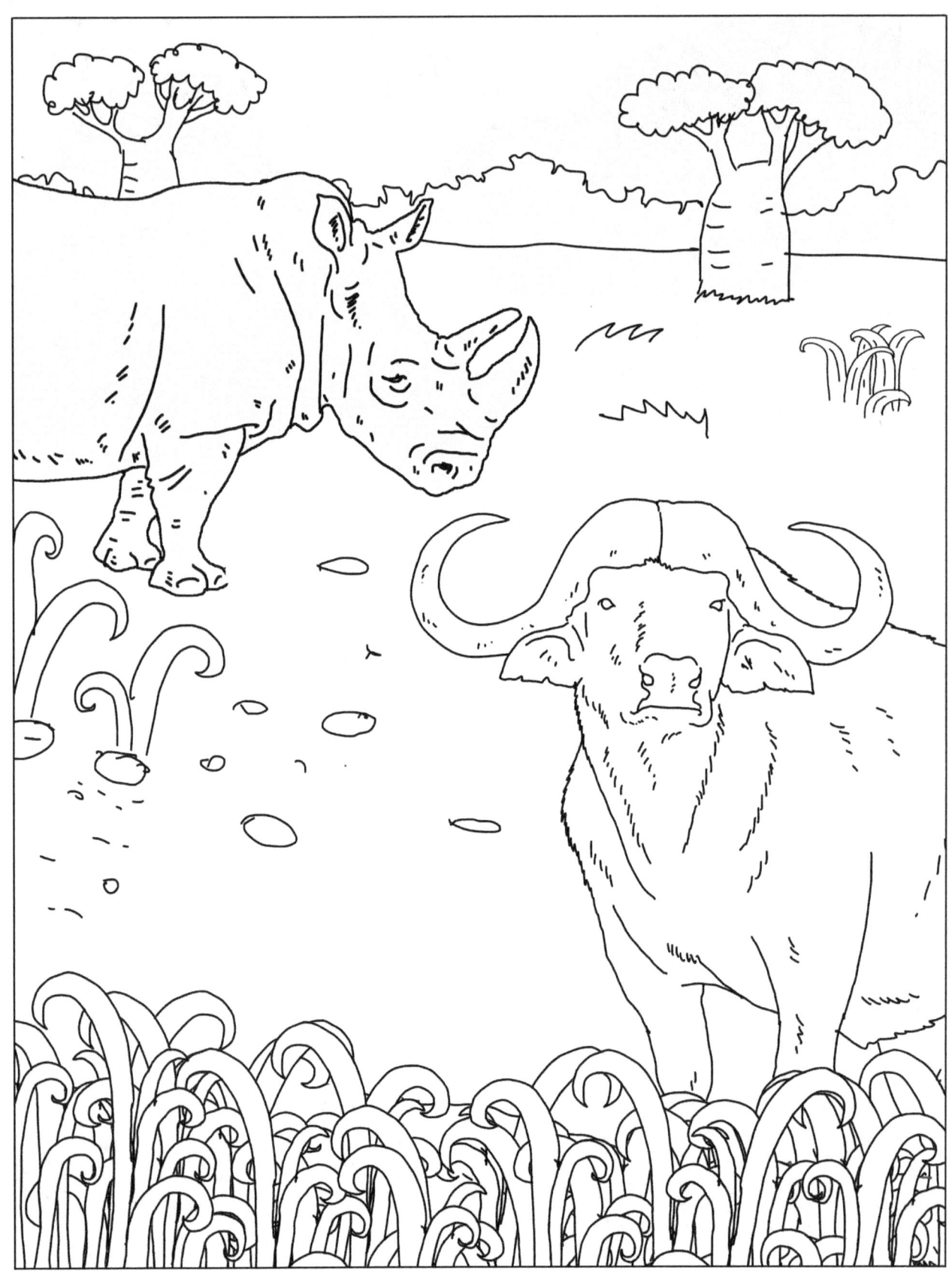

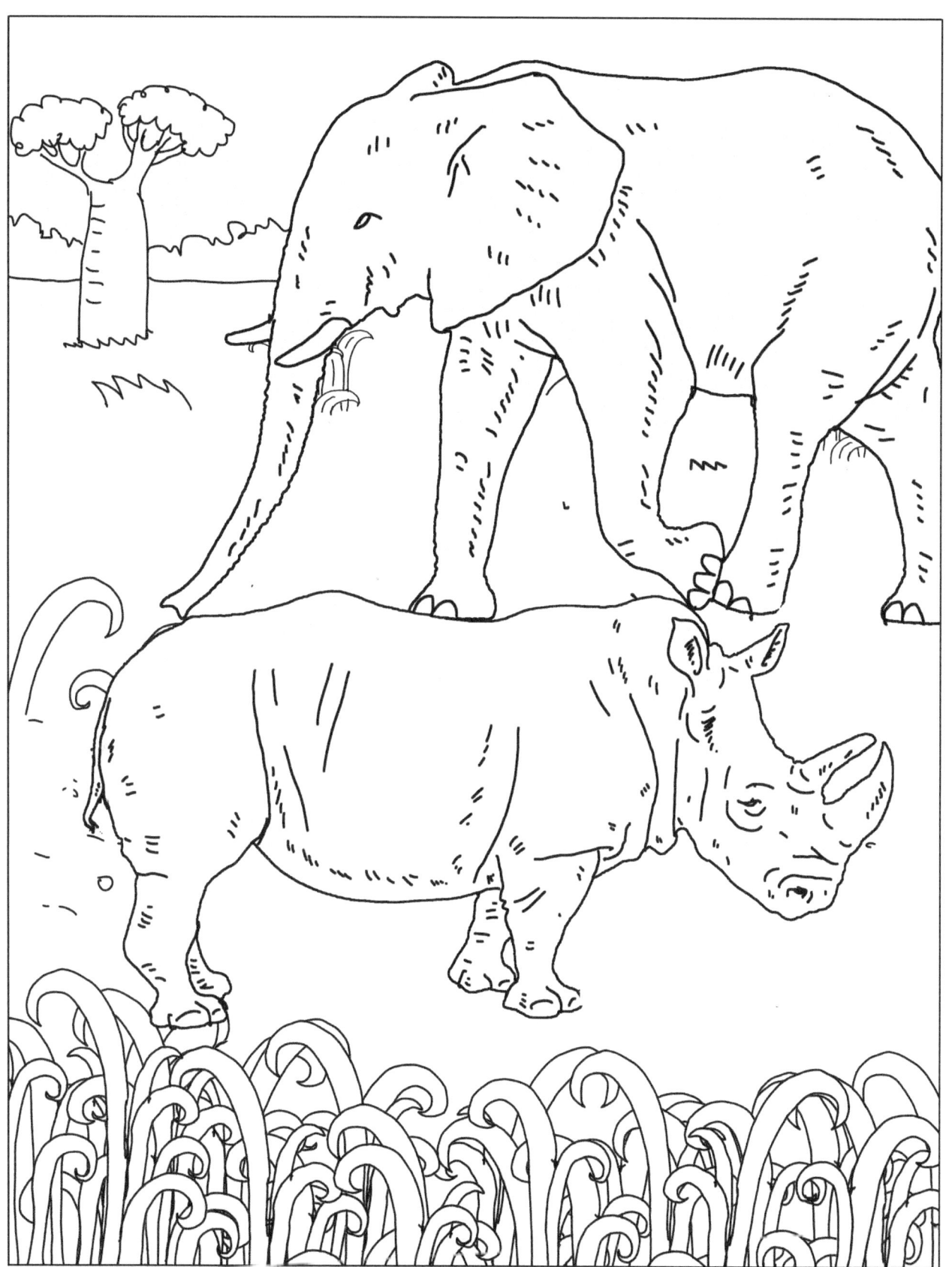

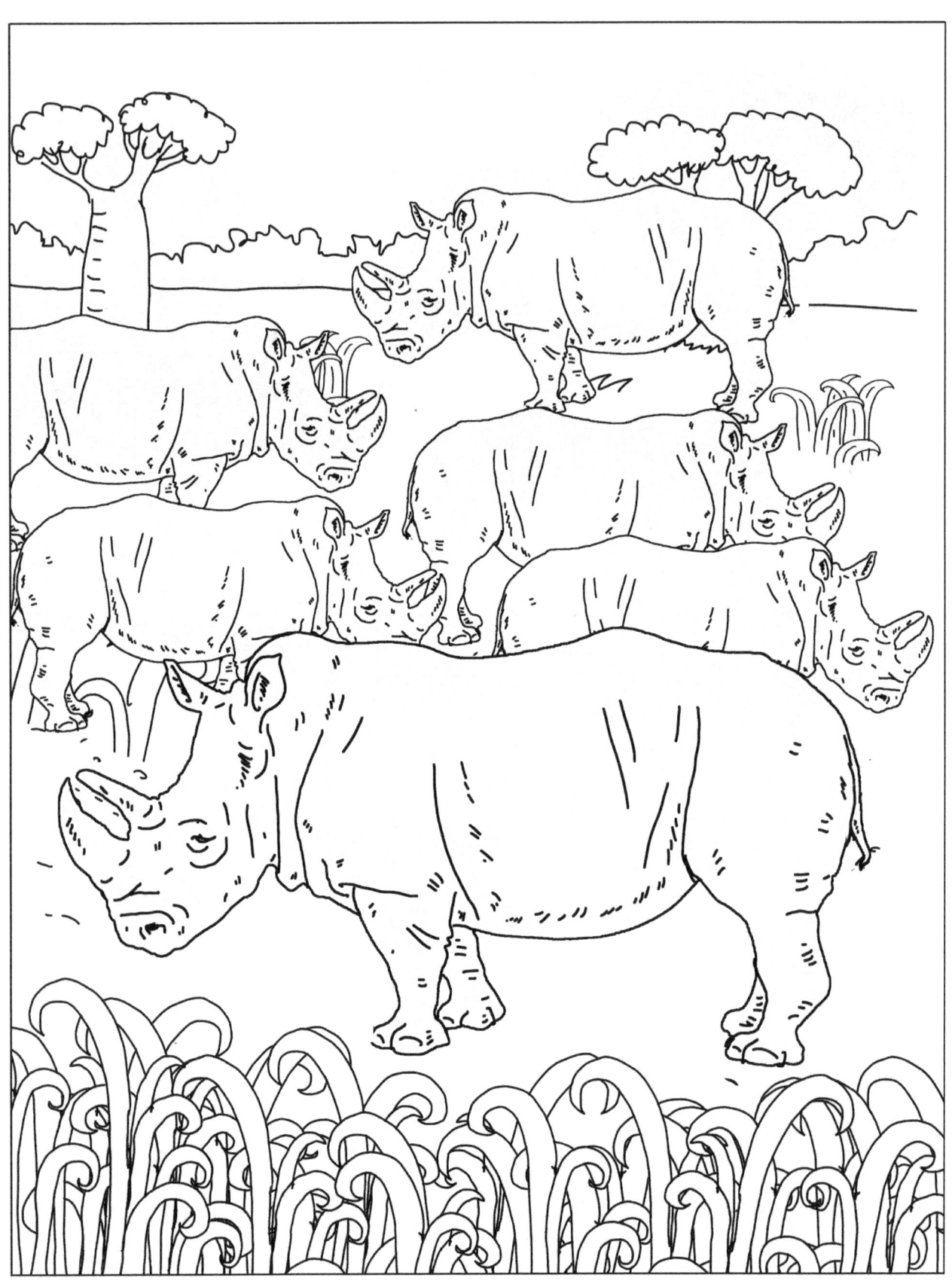

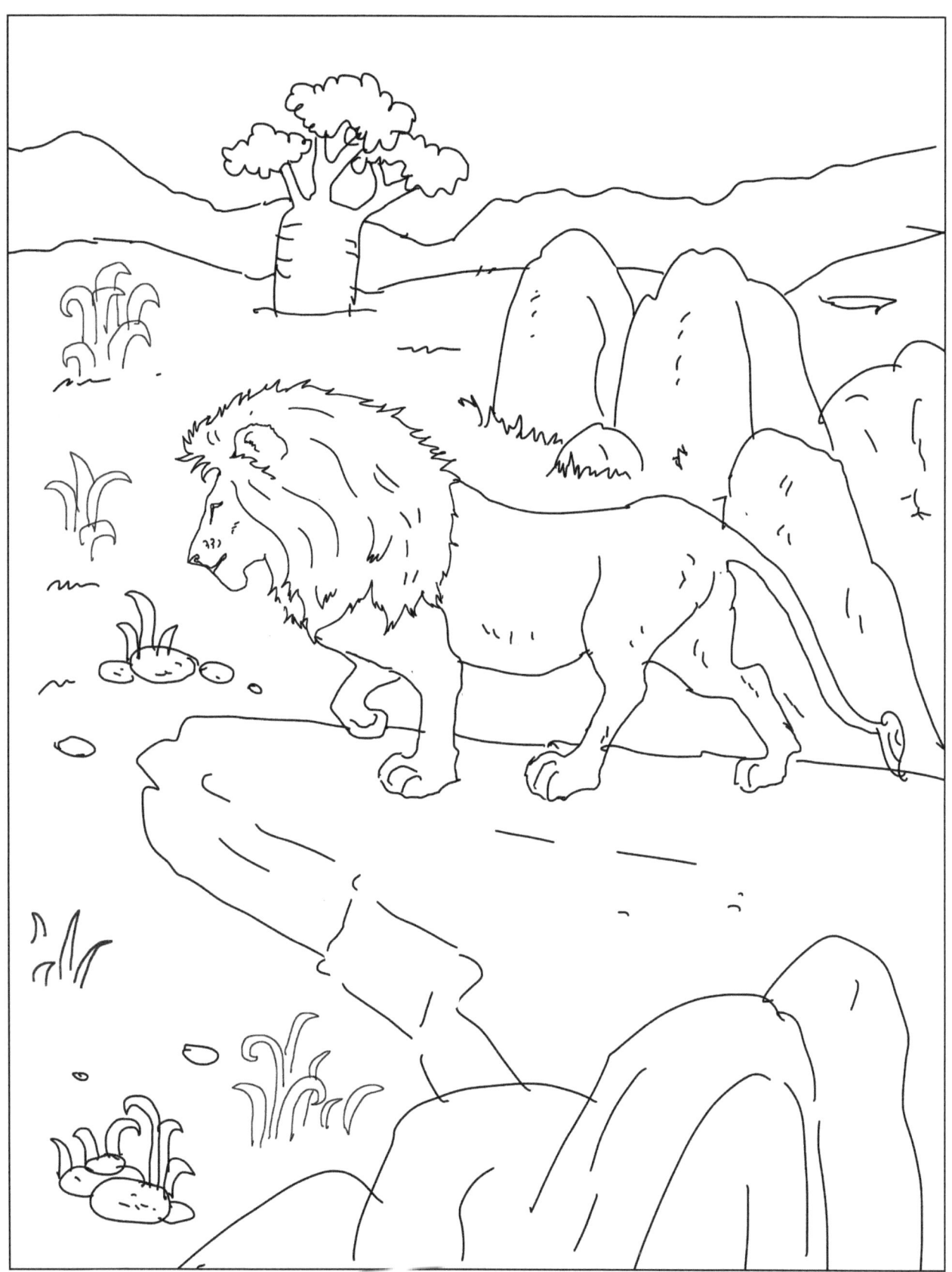

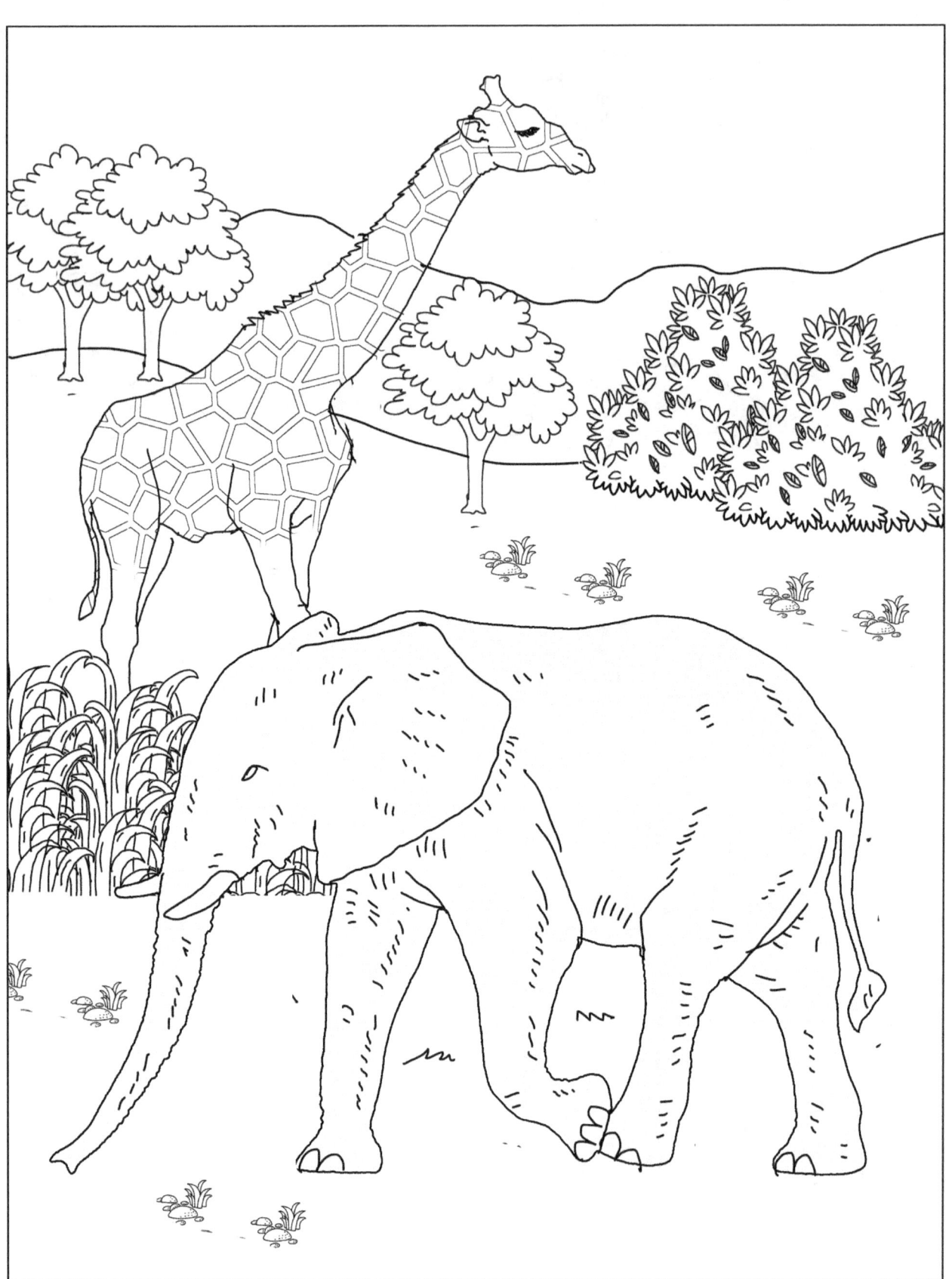

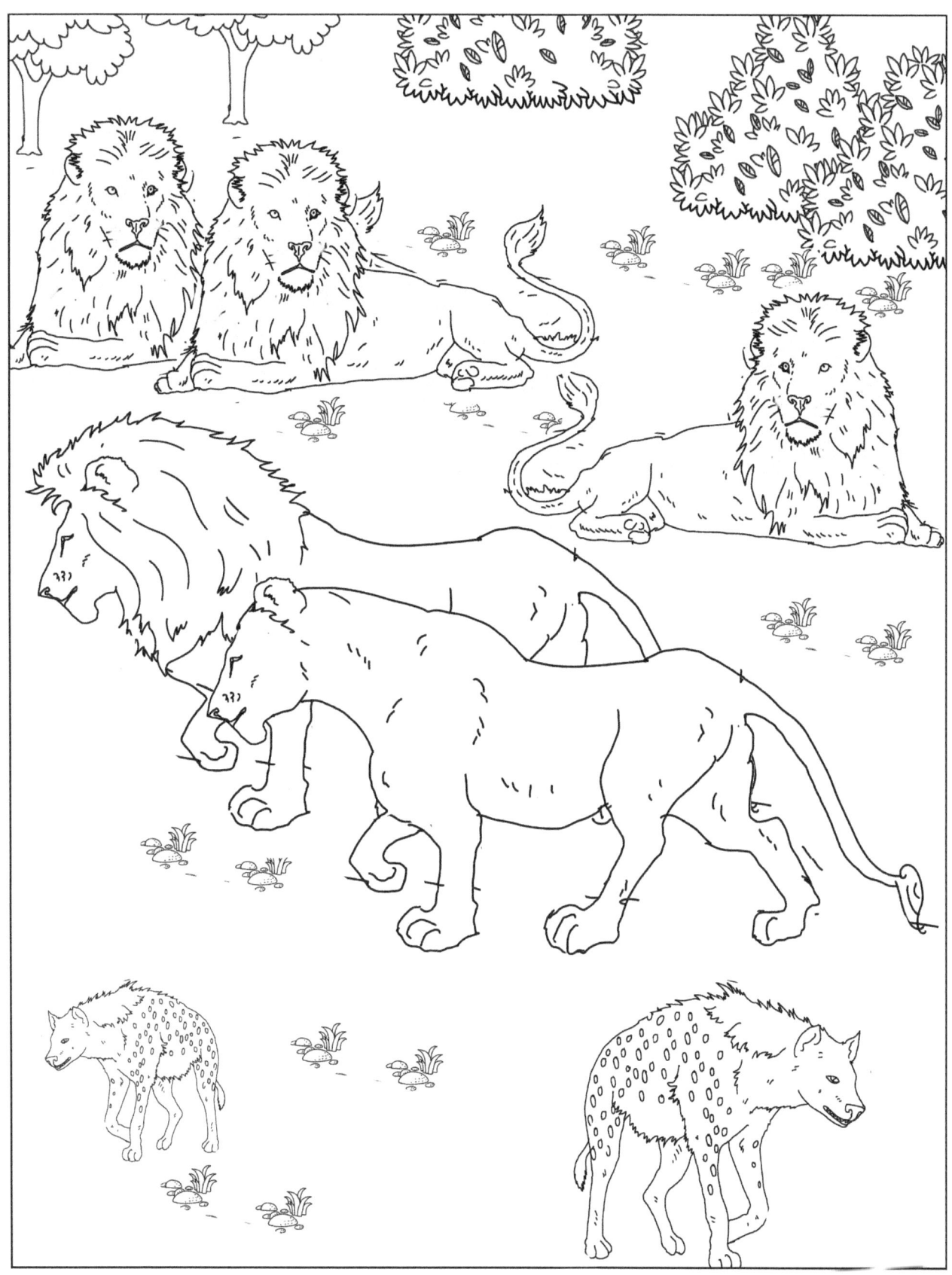

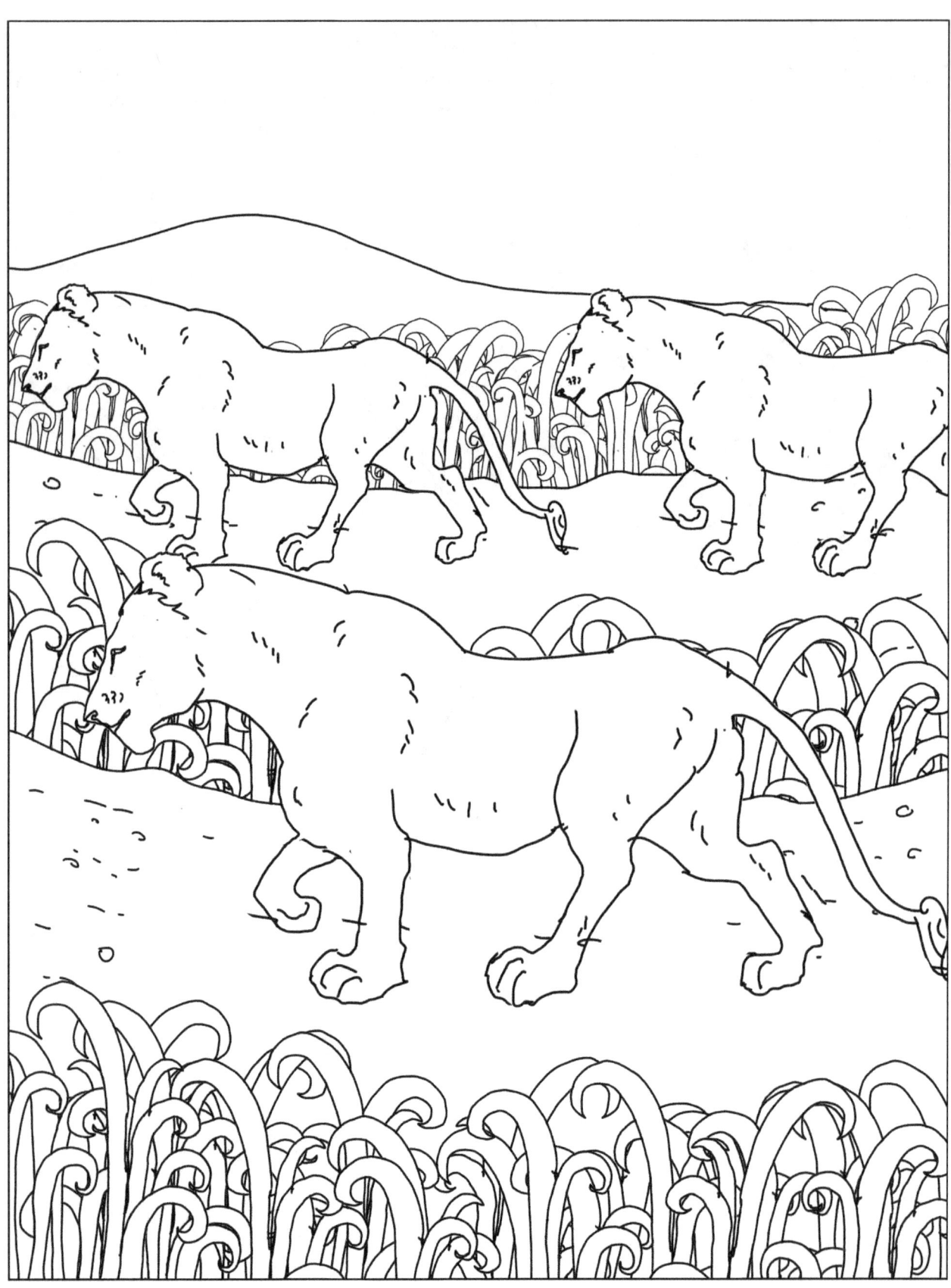

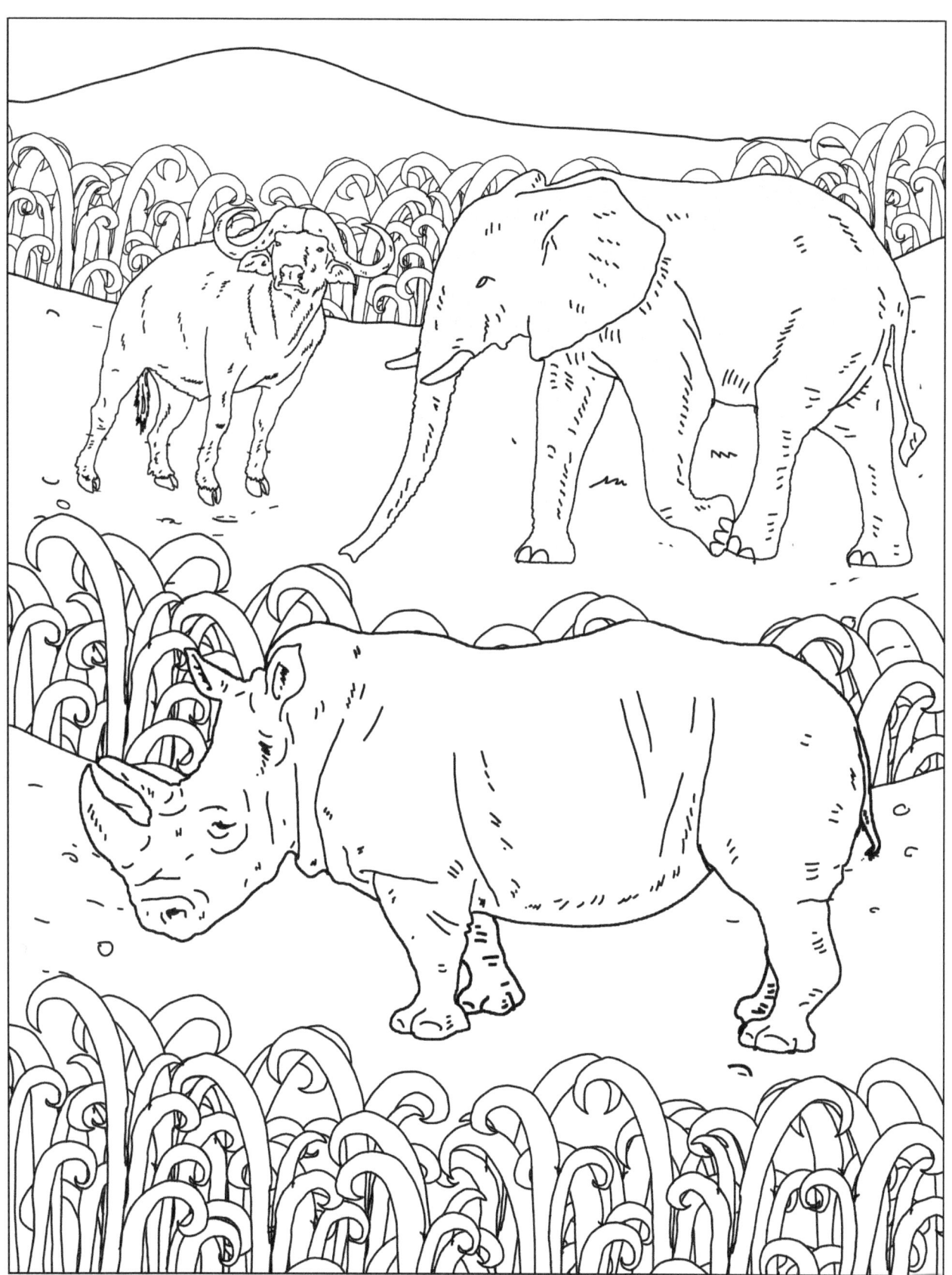

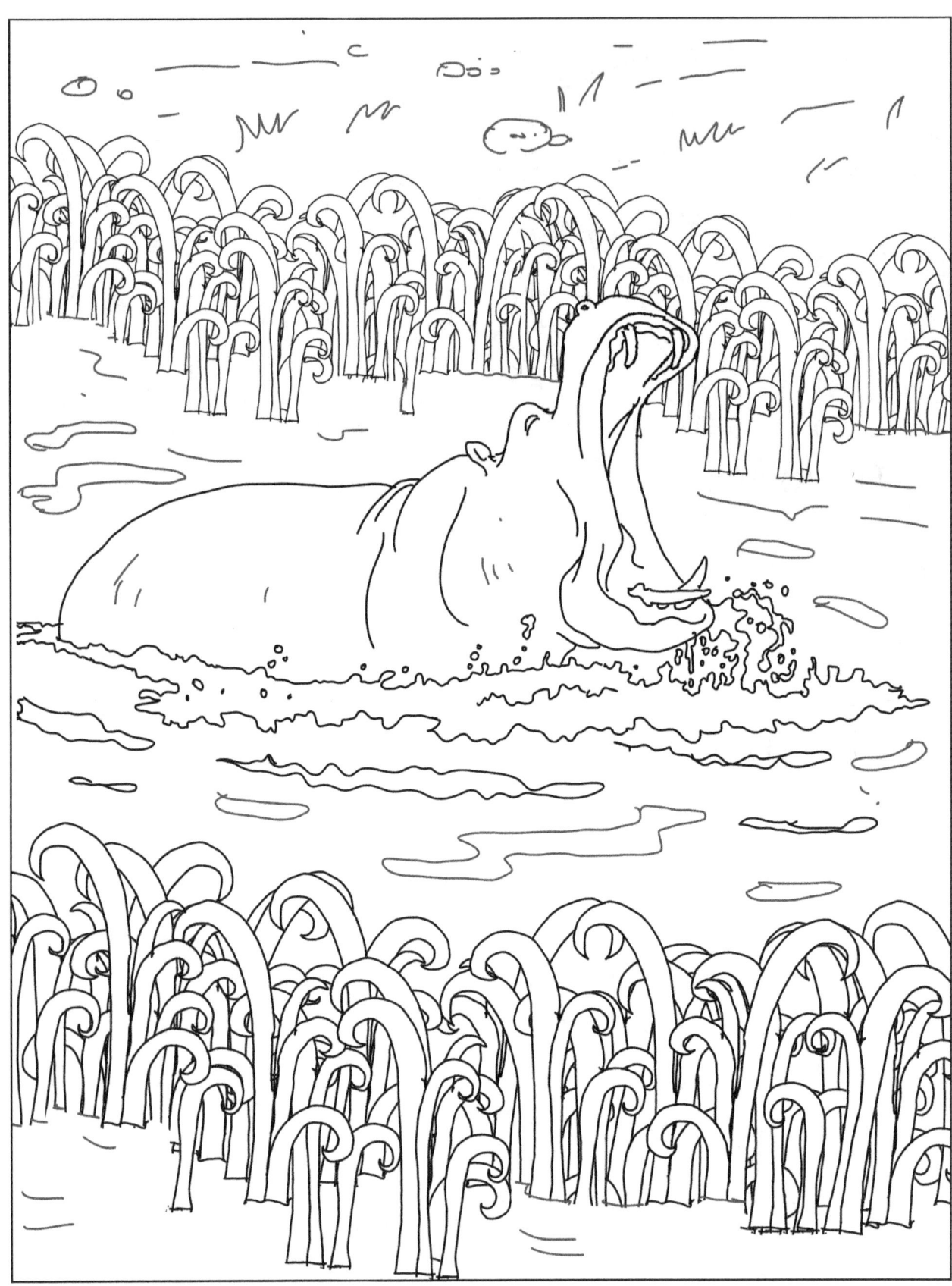

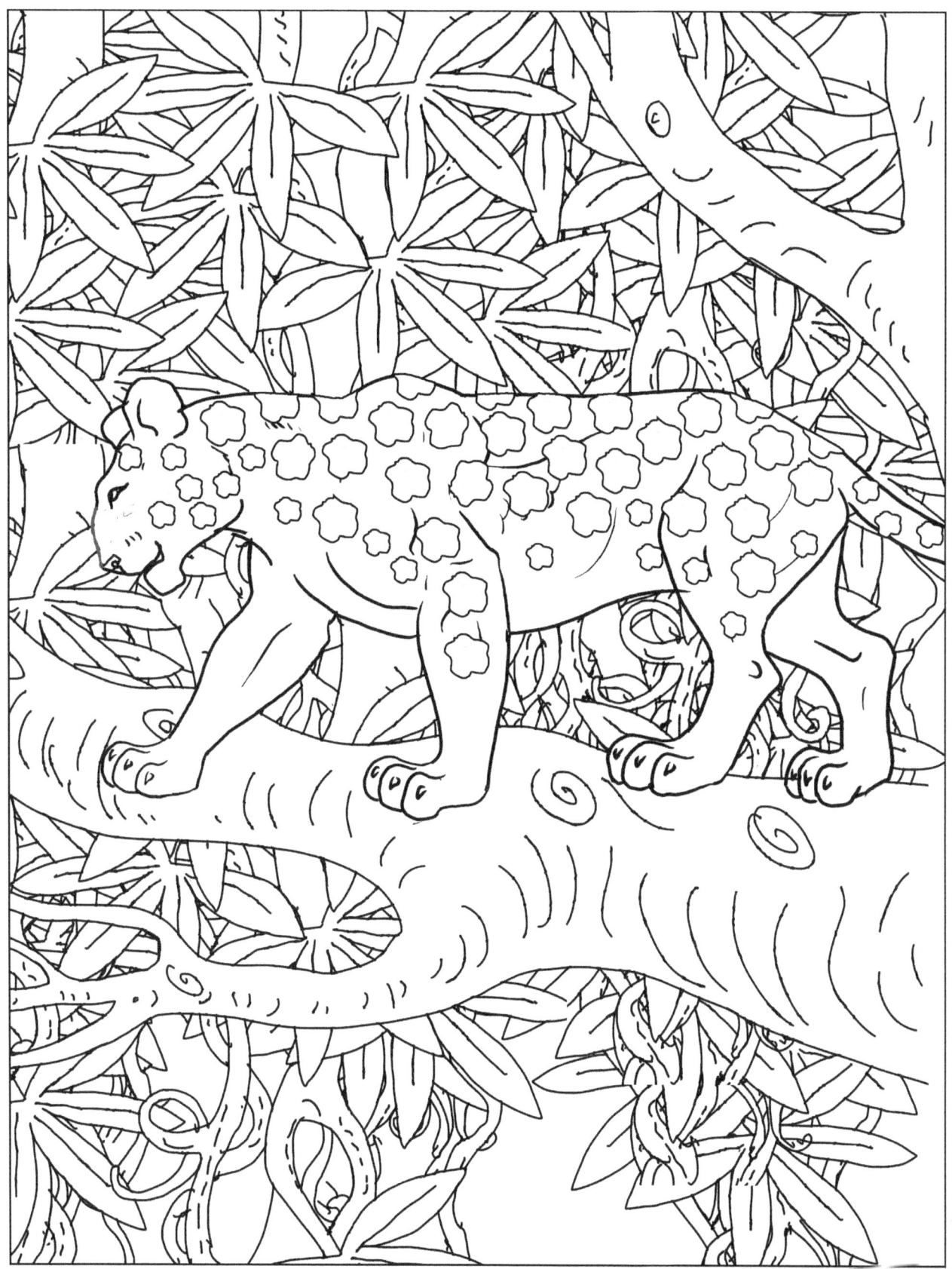

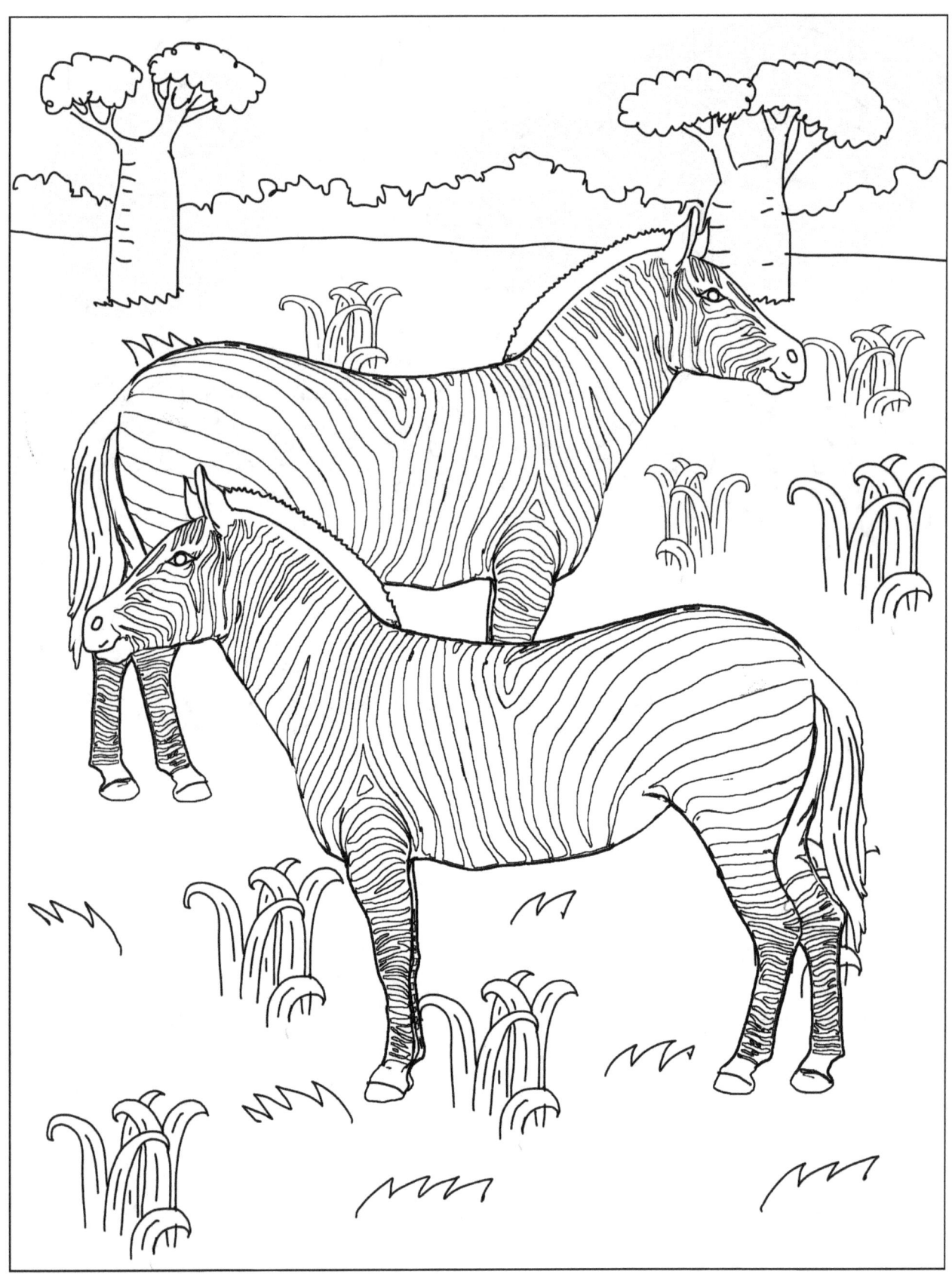

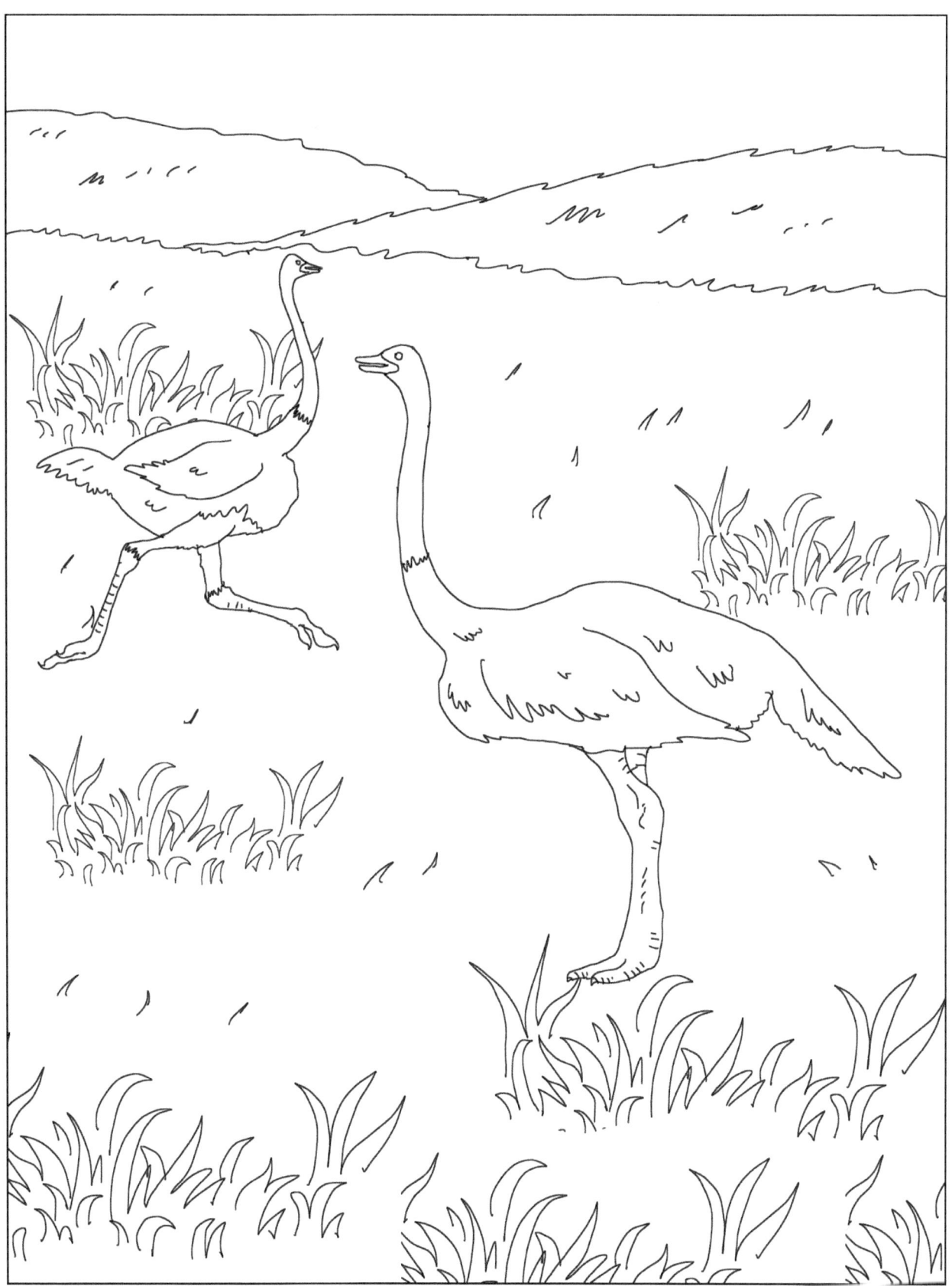

Thank You !

Bambang Wisudyantoro

cannonzhooter@gmail.com

www.ingramcontent.com/pod-product-compliance
Lightning Source LLC
Chambersburg PA
CBHW080533190526
45169CB00008B/3138